Acts and Intentions

pianta

Cover photo

Remains of Shuri Castle, Naha, Okinawa, World War II archive photos, Kelseyk1995, Internet Archive.

Table of Contents

INTRODUCTION

So many events in life –whether joyous or difficult–take a long time to process. At least, they do for me. Some I will never fully grasp. The intents and motives that lie beneath actions or events–whether personal or global– are complicated. I'm grateful for poems and the process of writing because writing can bring comfort or appreciation or joy, often about things that feel irreconcilable and unknowable. These poems are the result of trying to work things out and understand, and in some cases, to honor.

THE FIRES
Witch Creek, Harris, Rice, and Poomacha

small sticks start to shake from the trees

there's a bruise across the sky

branches crack
and the door keeps blowing open

the tangerines are still green
underfed by the drought

and a palm leaf
curls in the heat
breaking apart as it falls

the horizon is burning

and people drive into it

others hose their roofs
and those of their neighbors'

only to pause later before plasma screens
 in dark hotel rooms
to recharge cell phones that are dimming

some come home
to pull melted celluloid and picture frames

from liquefied girders

everywhere black dust flying

peppering eyes
while searing air compresses itself
under the grey insulation of sky

three days in

and the schools are closed
buildings are empty
only at 20% containment

water lines pulse like dying arteries
buckets of pink retardant
drop from the sky
veins of fire spider inland

as the world watches us burn

half a million are in the state of evacuation

firefighters in black smudged coats
march past 300 folding beds
which wait unused in hotel ballrooms
for them to sleep in shifts

instead they scorch their lungs

sleepless
as they hold onto the fire lines

days pass
as their own houses glow, darken, collapse

they save the city

in heavy boots they slosh
through water and debris called slash
with black flakes everywhere

they return to fall
into their narrow cots
having slain
the tetrahedron

the live body

of fire

ACTS AND INTENTIONS

Francisco de Asís Tárrega lost part of his sight
when he fell at four
and that melancholic poignancy moves
in *La Grima*
a lingering
you can feel in your fingers

we don't know what he fully intended
in *Recuerdos de la Alhambra*
beyond the Moors
or the castle

he couldn't have known that
*The Killing Field*s was to come—
that an aging rock star—
caught in a feud over a villa overhanging a cliff in Ibiza—
would adhere him to a film score that haunts us

that tinny waver of an electronic Étude
is juxtaposed against a Cambodian boy on a water buffalo
standing in ankle-deep green rows of rice

this is how we library the genocide of a people in celluloid

the story line lost
when Haing S. Ngor lost his life on a Los Angeles street

he refused to hand over the locket of his wife—

so he held on

murdered
because that last bit of her would not be given up

brutality
is just a breath away from our ear

when Dith Pran spoke
upon Ngor's death
he said he now felt alone

at the end of his life
Tárrega played for small audiences
cutting his nails
and striking the chords with his flesh

the world is known for its capriciousness
for deeds
violent, disingenuous or otherwise

these things I try to fathom

how a childhood fall led Tárrega to music
how his fluttering score eulogizes millions
how this was carried through his hands to mine

and how these notes are heard still

YUTA

Maternal Deities: Yasuo Higa Exhibition
Photographs of Ryuukyuu yuta, women shaman
Izu Photo Museum

in the absoluteness of black and white
and all the degrees between
Yasuo Higa photographed women in the sacred grove
thirty or more in a vast circle
dressed in crisp, ceremonial white cotton

through the exposure of light
we are witness
to women fully seated in their power

Kudaka Island, Fubo Utaki, Fubawaku, 1975
Iriomote Island, Sonai, Shitsu, 1974
Miyako Island, Karimata, Uyan, 1989
Irabu Island, Imonigai, 1995

there are so few people
I can tell about these photographs—
to whom they will matter

Higa photographed them
in the performance of their rituals
in some cases
lines of women
all in white

their heads completely obscured by greenery
as full as overturned bowls
layer upon layer of leaves
with only their mouths visible

late at night
when I can't sleep
I look at them

he couldn't stop
he went again
and again
over a hundred times
to capture them

I sleep better after seeing them
as if the fronds and greens
that they hold in their fists
can be called up around me
and that I might learn
what they know
and that I might feel
what they feel
in that sacred grove

UCHINANCHU

For Byron Fija
Wanne Uchinanchu – I am Okinawan.

show me the blood
and bones
the sacred grove
of women
and the miscanthus

the usurpation
of Uchinanchu "ni"
that became "ne"
in my family's name
A-ka-mi-ni
my father kept the pronunciation
whole and unbroken

but I changed mine without realizing it
in Japanese class
I gave it the "ne"
like the schoolbook told me
and just like that

a knot gets untied
the anchor rope
that secures us
that disintegrates
into filmy seaweed from years

of lying at the bottom of the sea

Uchinanchu
what is your culture

is it in the skin
of the taiko
or the purple fabric
dyed so deep
as to turn a river
dark as the strain
of DNA

the karmic
siren

that makes the fall of suicide
more palatable
than the shame of living

or is the culture in
the over 100,000 casualties—
men, women, and children—
nearly a third of its population
in the 82 days
during the Battle of Okinawa

or is it in the stacks of litigation
brought on by aging Japanese

who want essays of Nobel Prize winners
stillborn
so that culpability for suicide-genocide
remains submerged

already 110,000 in Ginowan have gathered
to light a fire of peace
and bear witness
denouncing as complicity
the removal of these criminal acts
from textbooks
rejecting the expulsion
of their truth

though less is said
about the Uchinanchu women
raped at the end of the war
documented by historians yet
no war crimes reported
military officials say

out of turbulence
come whispers
and a sudden plume of particles

that floats above shifting ground
shaken loose by the exhaling
of the Tohoku tidal wave

we find ourselves tied like buoys
to the Fukushima 50–
heroism complicates–
as they
encased in white
attempt the work of 800
while statements from management seep out slowly
like the micro-flecks
of radioactivity
that appear on spinach and
buds of chrysanthemum leaves

we call out to the criminal acts
that scar the body of the island

as it struggles against the vise
of military bases
the dark metal
of war

that attempts to propagate itself

as an industry
but instead

sours the water
and turns the stomach
acidic
and hurting

Uchinanchu

spread over land mass
and oceans
Peru, Brazil, Bolivia,
Argentina, Paraguay,
Hawai'i

are we now like the languages
we adopted
and our physicality as hybrid as the landscapes
we emigrated to
scattered from the archipelago that birthed us
existing only to reconnoiter

in odori
a dance to escape
churning water

wrists turning
as the heel pivots the floor

circling

to declare ourselves
nerve and bone
liquid and flesh

in the last strand leading
all the way
to the drum

of the moon

MINYO CRUSADERS DEMO IN THE MAIL

play selection #3 *Yasuki Bushi*
of the Minyo Crusaders demo
if you want Francis Ford Coppola's fifties Havana
overlaid onto Wong-Kar Wai's
In the Mood for Love
led by Uchinanchu
from the fields

it evokes high intensity color
—not vintage or retro or tepid fusion—
but a slice of the real thing

knock on that door
of a smoky club
where the races mix
after working in the fields
with brass wailing

where laborers
dressed in their best Saturday night suits
and women in tight sheathes
move and sing
dead from exhaustion and plantations
but alive and sweating
singing from the belly

be careful
when you crack this open

when it enters your ears

the vocalist's cat-eye liner
syncopates
with her lips

the packed sounds uncoil you
and the images lean into italicized
colorized silhouettes
sliding you into a saturated world
where visions
unlocked in the body
sing

REVOLUTIONS OF THE HEAVENLY SPHERES

the reburial of Copernicus

you wait beneath the ground in an unmarked grave
queued up for DNA and carbon testing
and software simulations for
facial features

on a headstone as black as onyx
they intend to give you
a sun and six planets
and you remember
the supine nature
of the woman you loved
and eventually gave up
under pressure from the Church
which remains in its moral tenor
essentially the same

but they bless you now with holy water
after spinning your theorem
like a hog
on a fiery spit

now cognizant
of the source of heat
and heliocentric order
they have cooked heresy
into a crispy
skin

out of chronological order
you now follow Galileo in this postmortem trek
the absolution for him having come years earlier
after he fell in the Inquisition
himself
excoriated
for the theories
he sprang

then like an aromatic drift
from the perimeters of the brain
a blank screen
of intuition rises
from which all brilliant bits come

but be forewarned now
of the perils of intelligence
and inherent curiosity

your brethren
have chosen
to rebury you
just as they reviled you
for having said what you said
the first time
around

TIBERIUS

you remain
in the mausoleum of Augustus
no longer on the Isle of Capri
a name that civilization will later use
to describe a calf-length pant
surrounded by bikini wearers
and pink-fringed girls doing the swim

this link to water is more than tentative
your name close to the river which is thought to birth Rome

not much can be discerned by studying your portraits
or reduced biographical descriptions
labeled a mere stepson

despite all this
you manage to appear in gold
"carnelian intaglio"
accession number
1994.230.7 at the Met

were you reframed
or exposed?

it is difficult to discern

your Rome as exploitive
as the media now

your legacy as undetermined and uneven
as celebrities caught in contemporary times
in acts unsavory

yet you have retained your power
in this acclimated room
you who remain inescapable

it's redemption we all seek
and you are fortunate
your advocacy delivered by a docent's recitation
into my waiting
uncertain ear

TO THOSE WHO STITCH FOR HAUTE COUTURE

to those on 6th arrondissement of Paris
and the House of Lesage
we salute you!

even today as the rest of the world ogles denim
and chooses the suffocation of synthetic over silk

you stitch
kilos of beads   and millions of sequins
365 days of the year

we are in awe
over the noblesse oblige of seamstresses

you remain in anonymity
in a sanctuary of sacrifice
as flawless as nuns
as you handle the immaculate expanse
of white bridal gowns
with your own white gloves

nameless, you
and your seed pearls rest
as illuminated

and cherished as prayer beads
in the cool air of the Met

I understand your sense that the work never ends
as the sound of my pen
attempts to mark crisp blank paper
as starched as linen

we both curve our bodies over worktables
and lose ourselves in tidy rows
liberated from everything
sequestered from life

immersed in our work
lost in the pulse
like the hunter
after the deer
absorbed in this pursuit
caught in the desire
to be a part
of beauty

YOU BROUGHT HER ONCE

I remember you brought her once
to a wedding

she was in a dark pink dress with ruching
and held a clutch as flat as an empty envelope
her eyes red from crying

the wife of a yakuza boss
—she was trying to get away—
you didn't desert her

sometimes we are all
wives of a yakuza boss
trying to run away with what we can carry
captured with our red-rimmed eyes
in ruched dresses
watching as someone goes down the aisle
while contemplating our chances
for getting away

I don't know if she made it or not
or whether the two of you made it or not
or whether there was ever such a triangle of fate

but it gives me pause
the tenderness in which you introduced her
and how she came to greet us
crying eyes
and all

I WANT TO SAY

I want to say
find a way to get healed up
but you're still
enamored with someone who gives you pain
and that's a hard
drug
to give up

you start to go through the withdrawal
the delirium tremens
trapped between
the hellfire
the ecstasy of what it was
and the uncertainty laced with what might come

the familiarity of grieving
feels more real to hold on to

it seems like a plus
to choose what you've already known

I hardly know you

you probably think
who is she
to tell me this

but I still want to tell you
these scars take so long to heal
and these veins so long
to clear

JUST FOR OURSELVES

words are sometimes intimacies just for ourselves
even though we didn't create them for that

we never know if a tender word
will be received or how it will be
so we lay it out
finely pressed
then fold it
and keep it in a drawer

sometimes we bury it
and say elegiac words
usually with ourselves sniffling into a handkerchief
under an umbrella in the rain

or in rare cases
we plant it like a seed
and promise we won't dig it up

we'll just let it grow
to see if it can burst
out of the earth
on its own sheer will
its tender flesh
made green and yearning

BY THIS TIME NEXT YEAR

this time next year
it'll be different
the tides will have detached themselves
from the body of the moon
and the water will express its own volition
to leave the shore when it wants to

the grief you feel
will be like all wars
no one will agree on what started it
and everyone will lay claim to what solved it

there are terrible things we do in love
that we pledge not to do
and we commit
to acts
to undo them

in this moment now
there is nowhere else to go

but by this time next year
it'll be different
the tides will have detached themselves
from the body of the moon
and the water will express its own volition
to leave the shore when it wants to

NEW

when my brother sat up
after four rounds of morphine
in intensive care
and asked
what time is it?

I had barely made it back
from my sister-in-law's collapse

why? I said
you going somewhere?

he laughed
the first real sound I heard
after they removed
the intubation tube

they said he would last
a few minutes
in the end
he lasted till spring
till the Ides of March

but there was joy in that moment
in that hospital room
replicating everywhere
so much light

there's a version of happiness you can have
after such events

I think about this as I drive home
trailing after cars and their taillights
allowing myself to give in
as we sway en masse
adhering to the curves

the tiny white lights of the reflector strips
embedded in the road
as demure
as beading in the houses of couture

yes
if you look for it you will find it
accession no. 1977.329.5a, b
catalogued at the Met

Yves St Laurent's transparent
l'elephant blanc
the sheer evening trapeze dress
with the hidden ribbed corset
appears effortless
but it's built to last centuries

if you look
you can see

how metal holds up bone
suspended with an airy grace

it's the way surgical units swarm and appear
then dissipate
like puffs of jelly fish that plump up
then disappear

tonight
my inhalations feel like
the only thread
holding me here
and the beaded lights of the street
the only source to guide me

but I know someone saved that dress to give to the Met
someone I loved woke up in intensive care
someone will notice this color
that I put to my lips

it's a strange kind of happiness
after the ICU ward
as frail as handstitched seams
barely held together
but there nonetheless

THE YEAR CRACKED OPEN

the year cracked open

and all of my insides came out
as beautiful as rubies
eviscerated
strung on long, long strings
but still there

I wanted to be the pearl
but ended up
blood red
and all the heart that goes with that

I was crying and begging on my knees
to have my brother live

but there are billions of details
both atomic and grand
petty and forgotten that determine these outcomes

once set in motion
they click like
the subway turnstile

or like the lock and load

we take what we can
then do what?

do away with what we can't?

I twisted and turned
until the new year came

over a field the first day rose
our family collapsed within itself
to fill the holes from the absences
of those who had left

how do we reconfigure?

bodies wind
and unwind themselves
unsure of what limbs are saved or lost

where they end
and someone else begins

I'm unable to articulate
the tragedies
or to say what keeps our vital organs intact

those pale, birthing rays of the first few days
let us know
we have fought through something

hardened into what was
beyond ourselves

something death couldn't burn
or cleave from our essential selves

we found a way to be quieter

knowing what it takes now
to lunge towards life

to feel a glance
to exchange a word

to have a moment
or a lifetime

to feel something as vast
or small
as the brushing by of someone
who feels

some kind of love

WHAT IT IS

it's a tsunami-like expansion
the heart breaks through its walls
flooding open beyond
what we think we can endure

we had a chance to love
and that person loved us
so we fall to the floor in gratitude

while the person is alive
if we allow ourselves that
it starts the tidal expansion now

the best thing is to go very, very quiet
and to allow all of that love
in
despite all

a friend told me when she was a child
in school in Japan
they were told to look at the clouds
and to use cotton
to shape clouds they saw over time
     she still remembers the names
     and the clouds
     she made by hand

can I capture what I truly love
the same way

shaping with fingers and palms
what I see in the sky

it escapes me
such matter
ephemeral
and fleeting

the souls as high
as close as far
as near
as I can
feel

ACKNOWLEDGMENTS

Much aloha to family and friends for all the love and support that they give, and a special thank you to Kumu Kapena and Kumu Lokelani. You share so much kindness and understanding with me and everyone. Much appreciation to Delaina Thomas and LeiHina Gibson for encouraging me to learn more about Okinawan culture through their own example. Many thanks also to the organizations and groups that work so hard to bring peace and cultural knowledge to the world. For those interested in more, there are notes and resources at the end of the book.

ABOUT THE AUTHOR

Pianta is a poet, fiction writer, and editor whose work has appeared in journals such as *Nimrod International Journal*, *Adirondack Review*, *Ekphrasis*, *Terrain.org*, and *Bamboo Ridge Press*. Originally from O'ahu, she has lived in California and North Carolina but has returned to the Big Island of Hawai'i. Even though her grandparents were from Okinawa, she only began to learn more about the culture as an adult. Her readings often incorporate live music, dance, and multimedia. Her projects include a children's CD and songbook, *Little Bird*, and a novella, *Old Volcano Road*. Her website can be found at www.pianta.org.

AUTHOR'S NOTE AND RESOURCES

Uchinanchu

I'm grateful to *Nimrod International Journal* for first
publishing "Uchinanchu" and for caring about these
issues. I read a powerful article by Byron Fija and Patrick
Heinrich, " 'Wanne Uchinanchu—I am Okinawan': Japan,
the U.S. and Okinawa's Endangered Languages,"in the
Asia-Pacific Journal: Japan Focus, November 22, 2007
and dedicated the poem to Fija because he is a devoted
advocate for Uchinanchu language and culture. The article
is a compelling piece and explains many of the conflicts
Okinawa faces. (Note, "Uchinanchu" and "Okinawan" are
sometimes used interchangeably, although the indigenous
term is "Uchinanchu.")

Preserving a culture has so many challenges. Uchinanchu
are sometimes viewed as "foreign," with less legitimacy
than other Japanese (who are referred to in Hawai'i as
Naichi*).* This makes saving a language and culture difficult.
Some of the obstacles are that remaining speakers of
Uchinaguchi are aging, attitudes about national identity are
unclear, and the protests against American military
presence bring their own divides.

The postwar arguments also continue. The high number of
casualties among Uchinanchu civilians in World War II,
and the causes for those numbers, continue to be
controversial. Nobel Prize winner Kenzaburo Oe was sued
by former Japanese military officers for his 1970 collection

of essays *Okinawan Notes* when it exposed the role of
Japanese soldiers in the mass suicides of hundreds of
Uchinanchu civilians in World War II.

In April 2011, Japan's Supreme Court upheld court
rulings that the Japanese military was "deeply involved" in
the coercion of mass suicides of Uchinanchu; as such, Oe's
work was deemed accurate and sales of *Okinawan Notes*
could continue. In 2007, in Okinawa, 110,000 protested
revisions in textbooks that removed mention of the
Japanese military's culpability in the mass suicides.

There is a line in the poem that says, "heroism
complicates." At the time I was writing the poem, the
Fukushima 50—fifty employees out of eight hundred—
stayed behind at the Fukushima Daiichi Power Plant to
stave off nuclear disaster. Acts of brutality and acts of
heroism co-exist within a world, a country, a family, an
individual. How does it all get sorted out? Is it through the
acts and intentions of individuals? If we continue with "us"
and "them," we perpetuate the same cycles that we're
trying to fight. At the same time, we have these histories in
us and ignoring them doesn't move us forward either.
Empathy seems to be a good starting point. Poems,
literature, art, music—maybe these things can help us try to
reconcile often highly emotional, divisive perspectives.

The context for that poem is also personal. I was born and
raised in Honolulu, but my grandparents on both sides
were Uchinanchu. They emigrated to Hawai'i to work in

the plantation fields. Because of World War II, the older generation, including my parents, felt they couldn't teach their children Japanese or the native Okinawan language, Uchinaguchi. For this reason, like many in my generation, even though I grew up in a multilingual household, I wasn't bilingual, nor was I curious about that as I should have been. I also didn't start to learn about what it meant to be Uchinanchu until I was an adult. I finally started to hear about this in an Asian American studies class at University of Hawai'i at Mānoa, and I asked my parents about their experiences.

These issues of identity and culture are difficult and nuanced. What I find encouraging is that people like Byron Fija—and others, whether Uchinanchu or not—are preserving whatever they can for others to experience. Many people grapple with their personal, individual identities and perceptions of reality, alongside issues of legitimacy and identity. Along with sadness, there is also a sense of discovery and appreciation for what remains and an optimism about what new generations will bring.

Other poems here honor those in vastly different fields, such as the seamstresses or the firefighters. The poem "The Fires" can't really express the devastation and panic that such disasters bring or the heroism of the firefighters. Those responders reflect genuine selflessness and nobility. What's tragic is the conditions for these events, caused by climate change, have grown exponentially. I find these things overwhelming. Writing a poem is a small act, but offering what we have, no matter how small, brings comfort, and that comfort keeps us moving, hopefully, to do more. It can help break down what's unfathomable into smaller, more actionable pieces. At least, that's my current strategy.

Part of what can keep us going are also the inspiring things people are doing in the world for the things they love. It's food for the soul, and we all need that kind of food—spiritual food—for encouragement. Here are some things I've come across, and I know there is so much more out there.

Resources

Hawai'i United Okinawa Association
https://huoa.org/nuuzi/

Center for Okinawan Studies
University of Hawai'i at Mānoa
http://manoa.hawaii.edu/okinawa/wordpress/

Ukwanshin Kabudan, a performing arts and cultural organization
http://ukwanshin.org/

Peace for Okinawa Coalition
https://www.peaceforokinawa.org/about.html

The Ryuku Kingdom: Cornerstone of East Asia

Mamoru Akamine, Translated by Lina Terrell and edited by
Robert Huey
University of Hawai'i Press

Women of the Sacred Groves by Susan Sered
https://www.amazon.com/Women-Sacred-Groves-
Priestesses-Okinawa/dp/0195124871

Maternal Deities, Yasuo Higa Photographic Exhibit
http://www.izuphoto-
museum.jp/e/exhibition/35835361.html

Far Side Music for ancient and modern Uchinanchu music
https://www.farsidemusic.com/

Power of Okinawa: Roots Music from the Ryukyus
An Okinawa-based music site
https://powerofokinawa.wordpress.com/

Okinawan-Brazilians
https://english.kyodonews.net/news/2019/12/008e46
e074c8-brazils-okinawa-descendants-hold-fundraiser-for-
gutted-shuri-castle.html

PUBLICATION CREDITS

"Uchinanchu," *Nimrod International Journal,* Fall 2019;
"Revolutions of the Heavenly Spheres," "Before," *San
Diego Poetry Annual* 2014 – 2015, March 2015;

RELEASES

Hawai'i Poems: from there to here
Collection of new and previously published poems
Available on Apple Books

Little Bird: Songs for Children
CD of children's songs
Available on iTunes and Apple Music
Samples at
https://pianta.hearnow.com/

Little Bird: Songs for Children Songbook
Accompanying songbook ebook at Apple Books.

Old Volcano Road
Novella
Ebook and print versions
Available on Kindle and Amazon

Before
Poetry chapbook
Available on Apple Books

Acts and Intentions
Poetry Chapbook
Print version on Amazon

The Secret of the Stem
Poetry and Prose Chapbook
Print version on Amazon

A Man in Parts
Poetry Chapbook
Print version on Amazon

Love and Grief in the Time of Ketu
Poetry Chapbook
Print version on Amazon

Short fiction

Floating
Ebook Available on Apple Books
Print version on Amazon

For more information
www.pianta.org